The Quotations of Bone

NORMAN DUBIE

The Quotations of Bone

Copper Canyon Press
Port Townsend, Washington

Printed in the United States of America
Cover art: Erika Blumenfield, *Light Leaks Variation No. 18* (*brief meditation on splitting light particles*), 2001. Type 59 Polaroids and clear push pins, 4.25 × 30 inches. Installation view from solo exhibition at Portland Institute for Contemporary Art (Portland, OR). www. erikablumenfeld.com
Copper Canyon Press is in residence at Fort Worden State Park in Port Townsend, Washington, under the auspices of Centrum. Centrum is a gathering place for artists and creative thinkers from around the world, students of all ages and backgrounds, and audiences seeking extraordinary cultural enrichment.

LIBRARY OF CONGRESS CATALOGING-IN-PUBLICATION DATA
Dubie, Norman, 1945– author.
[Poems. Selections]
The quotations of bone / Norman Dubie.
  p.   cm
Includes bibliographical references.
ISBN 978-1-55659-483-0 (pbk.: alk. paper)
I. Title.
PS3554.U255A6   2015
811'.54—dc23

2014030531

9 8 7 6 5 4 3 2 FIRST PRINTING

Copper Canyon Press
Post Office Box 271
Port Townsend, Washington 98368
www.coppercanyonpress.org

ACKNOWLEDGMENTS

"The Fallen Bird of the Fields" was published as a chapbook by Zone 3 (an imprint of Goldsmith Fine Press). Section 5 first appeared in *420pus*, and sections 6 and 7 first appeared in *Smartish Pace*.

The Academy of American Poets Poem-a-Day: "For Tranströmer" and "The Novel as Manuscript."

The American Poetry Review: "At First Sky in April," "August Storm before the Hippodrome," "The Butterfly House," "Homage to Sesshu (1420–1506)," "In a Western Siberian Wood," and "Last Published by Fire on the Pages of Lament."

Blackbird: "Again," "At the Tomb of Naiads," "Butter," "The Hat Called Sky," "The Quotations of Bone," "The Quotations of Meat," and "Sif Mons & the Messenger Birth Star."

Connotation Press: "The Boat," "A Military-Academic Complex," "The Post-card Alone," and "Wrong Sonnet of the Political Right/Left."

Conte: "The Jerusalem Moniker" and "Lines for Little Mila."

Crazyhorse: "'The Sparrow'" and "Ur-Dream."

Fiddlehead: "The Buddha on the Road," "Deuteronomy," "In the Age of the Mud-Toad-Leopard," "Speech of the Paraclete's Mouse," and "Winter's Grosse Fuge."

Gulf Coast: "Gotterdammerung."

Hampden-Sydney Poetry Review: "British Petroleum."

Hayden's Ferry Review: "The Crop Circle of a Country Parson" and "Prologue Speaking in Tongues."

Iowa Review: "Jericho Radio."

Matter: "The Last Light of a Quantum Plenum."

Memorious: "The Oral Tradition," "Telegram," and "Tiflis. July 1931."

Milk: "Shakespeare."

Narrative: "The Aspirin Papers," "Joan of Arc," "A Song without Words," "Under a Tabloid Moon," and "Winter Melons."

Passages North: "In a Matter of Adders."

Plume Poetry.com: "The Mirror."

South Dakota Review: "A Fifteenth-Century Bishop in His Mummy Cloth," "The Solar Famine of Hansel and Gretel," and "A Winter Window."

Spillway: "The Berlin Crisis" and "Yamantau Mountain."

The Superstition Review: "The Buddha on the Road."

West Branch: "The Conversation."

For my students

Contents

4

The Quotations of Bone

Prologue Speaking in Tongues

Sitting in the baked boulder field,
Jeremy called it a field of spuds, cactus tuft
rather than shavings of cheddar. The water
was good for this darker incline
of the Superstitions. The Dutchman says
one wing, one rock. You thought
Tagore's dress had a red pleated meridian
just below his breasts.

These holy men who make poems
with oil lamps disfiguring their faces, the nose
cleaved like a dead Venetian's slipper.
The lips
mocking a song of Cole Porter's...
easy to love. You said so, pointing
at the desert's full compass
because the world turns its circumference
into pond water's broken
golden mean. Abulafia?

I've refused to anyone say exactly
how, it a death, not the usual cribbage
or begging a difference
in socks...   gosh, I said
I do not want to hear it much
was clear of, Jeremy thought,
spuds. As if that could hurt anyone.
But it did.

1

I opened the window
like a vein.

BORIS PASTERNAK

The Fallen Bird of the Fields

I

She sings to the worms in transit
between the orchard
and the ghost-hurtling glacier,
the *ta sa la* of the stone dead,
but in passage
over a sack of coal
and the basket of seed potatoes.

It is the messenger bee, at last,
carrying a green and copper scroll
with the legitimate characters
of naked apostasy
written there in red and yellow pollen;
stone dead in the branches, the apples
have gone the beggar red
of a pomegranate.
Deer are grazing on the limestone ledges.

This is the cipher of everyone leaving us.
Not just with a fresh loneliness
but with those eyes of potatoes

for the only witnesses.

II

The red car crossed the snowfield
chasing a black bear. We ate
our tuna sandwiches—

III

with a dark beer and a shared cigarette
from Quebec. You laughed
because the bear ran while it shat. Something
you said that I would expect from marigolds.
The salad at the winter wedding.

Of your two breasts I favored
the one that was smaller—
that you deployed in a shameless act
of ventriloquism.

Just three short sentences in French.
And an almost polar totality
of punctuation.

IV

First the acetylene snow, then rain
blown across the black culvert,
again everything's cold
in deep-spun lockers

of spider loss,
the signing greek geometry—
It knows a sleep of helium
in stroking phobic realism: sunspots

on a dark blue plate. Your fever
relenting with the nausea. Starbuck

said these winter tapestries
always focus like the white fields on a red boar draped
from a long pole over the shoulders
of peasant men deploring
the children who are skating in the flooded medieval graveyards.

V. THE CHEMIST OF THE ZERO DOLMEN

The wind tugs at the loose tree line.
Dark skiers push through fog—
the snow adjusts its many shrouds
while blind sled dogs awaken beside the river.

NAS FUT 1012.0 ↓ 31.5. The birches
slice a dull sun.

An orange canister of bread crumbs
settles on the bottom of the river—
a laughter of lenses rinsing from glacial water.

The star threshold turns
its reversed letter.

The dream of the apothecary's dram
with a further half scruple
across a black sheet of paper. *Trakl*
with his dish of green tea. The obligation,
a broken ruby gammadion
with two methyl radicals calling
from the doll's house

across the hill
to Greta saying also

to the brother
that it's the eccentricity of the cone
that is killing Georg

little by little…

VI

Yes, Mother, it was a snowy day, Saturday.
I bought a new yellow dress. At night
I opened a cupboard and cans toppled out
striking me in the jaw
and left breast near the nipple. It's a pretty
green and purple now. I have
the cable on with the volume down
and Olivier, in a borrowed cloak, is wandering
among his men's campfires, an anonymous
droid. These men are
moody and complicated with bravery, rather
with thoughts that they might be dead,
or worse, on Agincourt's fields by late morning.

Suddenly I realized that these young and middle-aged soldiers,
these *actors,* as is the strange euphemism now
for some soldiers, I understood that almost all of them, busy
feigning a thoughtfulness about death,
are, in fact, *dead,* lying
there by their night fires with the lovely celluloid
blue lights on the hillsides. It was
depressing and I just walked off,
disgusted with this world, its actors,

to my kitchen bearing a large bruise in my breast.
I hear you laughing.
I'll write again on Wednesday. *Your daughter. Jean.*

VII

—Q was written before the war.
STEARNS

I limped down to the black canal
just to see a frayed red braid
of horsehair swim
among stars and broken branches
of paloverde. The sick
turquoise bellies of deadly snakes

changing, changing back in rain. I looked down to the distant
        101 Loop
where a dust storm caused a pileup
burning alive a man and his three children, the smoke
there since morning, a feint
or sleight off a coroner's cigar —   his
Cuban cologne over the father's
burst stomach with undigested painkillers
there like glistening fish roe, row
all your poor wooden boats
gently away from me, this old woman
crippled with a bitter affection
for these lost broken-pottery cultures
that dug this canal
a thousand years before the early morning
and the dead children

singing— *here comes the sun*—
for their mother's breakfast.

She's in bed with influenza.
Every cell in her body screams
at every other cell. And she smiles.
God help her always. It is
smoke-rise on Christmas day.

VIII

Well, Mother, again it is Wednesday. Beth has
been sulking since Christmas. I wish
I lived nearer to her. She seems
to think some frogs, all bats, the bees,
and a western snapping turtle
are soon to be extinct.
It is, it would seem, her anxiety
for *our* entire species. I said, yes—
well, good enough for us—   and
that's when she hung up. Since then
nothing but silence. I feel

we've lived through this before?

The A-bomb or Rachel Carson's birds
dropping in the wickets of goldenrod?
It's just so familiar. And boring as piss
that's stood in a pot from early evening
to late the next morning. Remember

what it was like in the '40s.
Sleeping in Alice Codlin's farmhouse.

12

From her blueberry pancakes with raw milk
to now our northern bats wearing a fungus
like a mustache of cocaine. *Flying out
into the winter with no fat.*
It breaks my heart. And Beth is

memorizing whole passages again
by the poet Trakl.
I fear she will be in hospital
by the weekend. She learns

both Trakl and the market sheets.
She says our brother's advances
were dressed in silver foil and vaseline.
I'll write on Monday.
Love. Jean.

IX. FEBRUARY 12

The snow folds
through the fences to the boathouse—
under it all
a canvas shoe and the broken oar
I threw at you last April.
Our mother insists you cannot
keep a secret.

Not even with the potatoes.
A shadow in the pines
evaporates in noon light.
And the rattling pie tins strung
around the springhouse
give me a shudder in the wind.

The fog has settled
down along the empty blue line
of birdhouses
that kneels at the frozen creek.

I remember you bathing there in late March.
Your face and chest were scarlet. There were
birch strikes across your buttocks.

Then three deer ran by and you sunk
backward into the snow.

The violence promised in Iran
sent my thoughts
off looking for refuge in the creek
and there I remembered your bath.
The deer. And that
children, thoughtful children, everywhere
on the planet are being tortured at this moment.

  x

She said something to the effect
that the horse
fell through the ice on the pond.
I said—   *no,*
no cheap thrills, please. We are
all aliens here.

  XI

  …in the flooded medieval graveyard.

XII

My dear, it is past Monday.
I am sorry for my silence.
But Beth broke hers…
She's returned to her future bed
to sleep with the stones. She
talks of orange caterpillars,
plums, and, of course, aliens
walking among us.

I say nothing, often. Being
the trusted sister.
And then I say
I have no doubts.
She pauses. Coughs.

Brags on the size of the brown trout
she's just raised frozen
from the outdoor locker.
I cleaned it for her
back in May and made my last
wedding salad that evening—

with butterscotch pudding.
And, yes, the fish was, of course,
another of her cruel anniversaries.

I pretend to fewer and fewer memories.
It doesn't punish, but makes
a clearing. In the mind,
the throat, the field.

She remembers nothing—I caught
that goddamn fish myself,
practically with a clothespin.
I love you Mother. Goodnight.
Your silly daughter. Jean.

XIII

I'm just an old woman
speaking from the far room

about the dandelions
being blue, not green
with yellow danglings…

       The killers
of Justin Marie Booth
never mattered—
Justin never mattered. He was
martyred by men in black pajamas.

It must
have been a dream.

Justin thought he never
dreamt, *there,* in Vietnam
except that first night of a late "offensive"
when our dead father
pulled another woman's long
blonde hair from a jelly
sandwich.

I think he must have dreamt

when straddling that white goat
in the narrow paddy trench. Dead,
the medic, Frenchie, told us—
just as Jean slapped

him silly into his next war
there in a rotting trailer outside Worcester.
She regrets it even today.
She says

wars of the maritime
must have been pretty?
I believe she was me that day.

XIV. THE LANCASTER LIVERY

When I was a little girl
witches from small painted towns
with giant pulp mills
were decidedly hungry. They dreamt
of old men
washing their faces in yellow grass.
The aunts are sweeping the pond
of snow. Their strong backs
working in tow with the south wind.
They laugh

at the further idea of us
and our desert high country.
The pink-and-black-banded snake
laughs at the aunts
so they take its skin
as a presentiment to the overt witches
who regret not eating the snake.

Commerce between
these sisters is a daybook
Fyodor Mikhaylovich Dostoyevsky
thought he lost
in a cold outhouse by the Baltic Sea.

This was pure dementia.
But the meat of the snake was eaten
by a black dog with white socks
who forgot to pause, to breathe,
so he suffered laryngitis
all that week—
finally barking a conviction
at a funeral procession that went down Elm St., dark
idling Studebakers
bumper to bumper for three miles. The stink
of pulp mills, father said,

is a Russian summer of old cabbages fried
a second time in horse fat.
It is very inert after that…
Dostoyevsky telling us
it all ends in a world of symbolism
with a dog barking at a dead woman
in her long cortege.

XV

Mother. It's simply that I watered your violets,
and they died. Their life
as straw cadaver
is small and tarnished.
It's been three years since you passed
and I am still writing

to place you between me and Elizabeth. The barrier mind
among sisters who worry not
the unlikely extinction plot
except for an occasional black turnip
that says…NOT…
not at supper or in front
of aliens. *She is adamant.*
They are from the constellation *Lyra?*

XVI

And why not. Enough of her. Sure, losing
at canasta in the probable spirit world
is like an improbable gob of bloody spit
on a hot clean sidewalk in Prescott, Arizona.
We are surely all lost.
                              Postscript: I know
I am the one
who wears black vests and visits hospitals
between semesters; *with all regrets your*
daughter, Jean. (Not in front of aliens, indeed,

XVII

and how it's been six months now since
she hung herself in the flooded basement.
I stood there and called her a cow. I was on the stairs.
I went *moo-moo* just like the Hindus.
I suppose it was some comfort
to what fish were below me there
in the foul creek water.) *Once, and again,*
your daughter. Jean. Woman, and what
about your husband?

XVIII

We watered him too. And
he died. I know — *Mr. Booth,*

sometimes, I think —
this is a fifth-rate planet.
Then, I exaggerate.

XIX

Sixth-rate? I'm dying too.
And the long count has nothing
to do with it. It's the vessel
in the shorter leg. The smaller breast.
The sappy
woman who administered my mammogram
is dead too. Mr. Hazlett said she was
nearly happy in the end.

XX

                    Moo. I went to middle school
with her cousin, June.

XXI

               Moo.

June 18, 2010

2

Love has no body and presides the sun.

JOHN BERRYMAN

British Petroleum

for Laura and Danny

A pollen link twisting in wind, the weak
purpling of salt urchins
and the sheath of the sea
itself printing certificates—
it is a malady of time
opposing mass, mass
hastening the gull to the horizon.

A line of Chinese characters
orbiting in ink, the minstrel sleep—
the body of Hart Crane washing up
on a white beach in the Yucatan. Peggy Guggenheim
has scrambled eggs with goat cheese
and there were fresh dates in the muffins.

Yet, he leapt into the gulf in blue
pajamas.

Yet, he leapt into the sea. It is
a classical difficulty for a bird reflected
in water, for water
reflected in the sky bisected
by the gull who plunges into the sea.

It isn't ink
we repeat in…   It isn't
mollusks whitening beach scree…
it's the city, it's night ark
gone alphabet with quarks
    entering the impossibly strange intercessional dark.

The Postcard Alone

the boy crusader, saint francis
stooped in his vest of three-penny nails
sits at a dark card table of lacquered azure
awaiting the wounds of jesus
while sipping a black tea with the holy turkman, future
sutures infecting
like fat around the trusses
of a baked goose, soon
the moon delusional
sequesters the simple tune
a yankee-doodle last day,

and war without taxes,
a volcano, the bishop's stroke,
fever and the winter sabbath,
stroke the young arab girl, death and max's,
the doge, a golden buick,

more whores, lost scarred sine
of protons, cook's stargate closing,
not a philosophy of rain,
the one and the many —
earthquakes again with a turk,
a bluish starched shroud,
a frayed cuff,
assisi is a long way off, a bridge
broken with lanterns —   surely
a Saint, it was not enough…

The Novel as Manuscript

An ars poetica

I remember the death, in Russia,
of postage stamps
like immense museum masterpieces
patchwork
wrapped in linen, tea stained,
with hemp for strapping…

these colored stamps designed for foreign places
were even printed during famine—
so when they vanished, so did the whole
Soviet system:
the Berlin Wall, tanks from Afghanistan,
and Ceauşescu's bride before a firing squad.

It had begun with the character of Yuri Zhivago
in a frozen wilderness, the summer house
of his dead in-laws, his
pregnant mistress asleep
before the fireplace
with flames dancing around a broken chair, piano keys,
and the gardener's long black underwear.

Lara lying there. A vulgar fat businessman
coming by sleigh to collect her for the dangers
of a near arctic escape…

But for Yuri, not that long ago, he was
with celebrity,
a young doctor publishing a thin volume

of poems in France, he was writing
now at a cold desk
poems against all experience
and for love of a woman buried
in moth-eaten furs on the floor—

while he wrote
wolves out along the green tree line
howled at him. The author of this novel,
Boris Pasternak, arranged it all. Stalin would
have liked to have killed him. But superstition kept him from it.
So, the daughter of Pasternak's mistress eventually
is walking with a candle
through a prison basement—
she is stepping over acres of twisted corpses
hoping to locate her vanished mother…
she thinks this reminds her of edging slowly
over the crust on a very deep snow, just a child who believes
she is about to be swallowed by the purity of it all,
like this write your new poems.

Telegram

Baudelaire's draft of pepper trees
and large deer asleep in snow—   a cosmic raft
burning above the night hill.

A card trick with a district mistress,
the purposeful syphilis, ancient
orbs of flowers fold—
sentimental,

resting on wet newspaper
but not with winter rains—   not Paris.

Chère, Great Danes

                              eating your black shoe.

Deuteronomy

Joe died of a disease of wheelbarrows.
Not the clashing of circles in a glad
and biblical sea. Not coughing,
and sneezing in a brief of roses.
No open punk sores. A galloping
in the ears of men
with black sacks over their heads. And a death
of one wheel.

Cold tea in Rhodesia.
The raw beet
is a plutocrat among boiled potatoes.
Hot tea
along the lake.
Of course it all worsens.
Uncle Joseph's coat has many colors.
Two knuckles of a brass hinge. Joe

Strummer died opening a door. Mourned
in the captivity of wheelbarrows.
Our new war now dedicated to the mining
of lithium on a narrow road
north of the Khyber.

It worsens with the tea.

The oars breaking in the key of C.

Lines for Little Mila

Here, in a cloud of rising flour
she dabs at her chin—   aging
leaves a blemish just like this…
the egg behind the cloud
of flour now falling
to a black mica counter.

Grandmother with a coffee tin
full of raw milk. The sun
gone beyond the mountains
long before it's gone from us.

Men cleaning fish, husking
corn on the porch.

I told a friend's little girl
about some of this,
and she immediately
slumbered, putting
a blue ghost inside my chest.

I said to her—
so you still remember things from the other side?
Then quickly I added—

of that river?

The Jerusalem Moniker

This gangster of an olive tree
had, at sunset, an old horse
for a girlfriend—named
Francine, spelled with three *n*'s...

This, like peace itself,
was permitted during, as I said,
the period of the sun's setting,
one bright sabbath evening
in January. Winter affections

are nothing but impossible detail.
There was just enough time
for some small intrigue and scandal—
Francine was with child
and an olive tree was rumored
to be the perturbed father.

Actually, that old fart
Samuel Beckett knocked up
the poor horse in a cool dark shed
in Palestine.
That's Palestine with two *n*'s. Don't forget it.
The authorities will question all of us in the smart set.
The gum and lambskin
prophylactic failed. I warned you—
it's the details of winter that upset us.

Wrong Sonnet of the Political Right/Left

Richard Nixon, laughing gas coloring his lips
blue with white blotches, is
exchanging, in this dream, worn socks
with me. He is also passing
stacks of gold coins to a mechanical panda
who tosses the coins into the skeletal lap
of an empress dowager. Nixon muttering
governing ain't pretty.

Depression-era green glass
flying past this Quaker statesman
whose brothers are bleeding at the mouth
much like the dowager who holds
the dripping hide of the panda
which she peeled off
with an element of grief
and a dull pear knife and her wooden teeth.

The Berlin Crisis

for Rebekah

Just another fake apocalypse with a white train moving slowly
through the snows of a mountain pass—
beyond there is the frozen lake
of mirror glass:

a weighted half of globe
slammed down on my pillow
by a small sister
just to say: *Wake, brother, the Great Dane*
has done a dirty on the rug
and Janie thinks it's as big

as the rope on her father's boat.
I say, "Shit!" And she giggles,
"That's right," skipping
out of the house
onto the green lawn with friends.

The Hat Called Sky

for Baatar Galsansukh

First, the firemen dressed in canvas
then the smoke
scribbles dead birds
before your eyes, who can know
the arc of killdeer
from the thunder-vise of aortic cataract—

the oxygen bright starlight in the brain
drains, the early Protestant comedy of delayed surprise,
complicates the eyes
rolling back while the head
likewise falls into the squash basket.

All of them as if in congregation
standing up with hymnals blanking their faces—
the dead lamp with its nib of black tongue
lollygagging the Mistress's planet
Mars setting with a full moon over Palestine.
Elmer Fudd eating crisply an eternally orange carrot;
little blind-bling miltons
moving sideways like crabs at his feet.

All our religions increasingly unworthy
of Thee
                    like a stranded cat in a tree.

Joan of Arc

You were almost still a young girl
staring at a dead horse
who had broken its leg
in the freshly painted yellow garden —   then,

you asked no one
for an explanation, thinking
all experience is frozen, of
the moment, of
the instant when two pale breasts
fall from a black sling frayed at the edges —
well, not quite, but again
of that moment and serial

like gunshots. Unless, of course,
it all occurs
in the one mind of being; or is
pushed like a string
by lamps of projection
against some neighboring vacuum,
a friend's big silvery Mercedes,
the smell of macaroni
boiling with the baby's black diaper;

or, again, perhaps just rising
from the immersion in Void
but no longer distant
from us in time and space. (The gunshots echoing
across the lake,

what separates the horse from its suffering,
like your fork weighted
with pink birthday cake.
The horse's leeched and flaring gums, a
memory with that strike of fern ridge
serrated by a hundred dusty marigolds,
the poor animal's enormous bowels
emptying onto a cold darkening beach.

The Quotations of Meat

It might have been the dead cow,
in dream, who said—   or the Tao
Te Ching—   it might have been the bow
of the boat, rising plough
in a storm-dark field, a spotted sow
and one barking dog? The Chairman Mao
said it—   now
is a time to try the soul:

peasants planting
seed with long gray poles…
it might have been the dead Angus
who said, a hamburger
seems the invention of cowshit
largely drying beside mushrooms
and the brook. The dead said it. It was
a little red book.

The Quotations of Bone

for Marvin

The meal of bone was a soured milk—
just the heads of giant elk
in a dark circle looking down
on a wooden bowl of soda crackers
and pork. One large knife
resting in the meat
of a woodsman's calloused hand.
He grins at his woman
who is slowly poisoning him
with the stringy resins of morning glory.
A tasteless turpentine with pink pig.
The speeches of bone
are matrimonial in early autumn—
by January there's a froth of blood
at a nostril.
He thinks a long icicle is buried in his ear.
She thinks D.H. Lawrence was a grim buccaneer.
I hate most men. Adore the few named Lou.
One small addendum:
the dead elk are grinning too.

3

Winter's *Grosse Fuge*

Take this, Da ist der Wisch, *& stuff it.*

BEETHOVEN TO HIS LANDLORD

I

Mrs. Mendez
go across the lawn to the firehouse
and tell them the old maestro
has collapsed—   clutching his head,
the left eye bulging with a hemorrhage,

saying he saw an Indian mural:
in the upper corner
dogs in snow were ripping
apart a doll of corn silk. A lost mural,
he said. My daughter
thinks he is now listing. Can you imagine?
Wild dogs, he said. Not wolves.

My daughter
screaming he's dead,
a squash blossom in his mouth.

II

He wanted no misunderstandings.

In the dream
it's the bath he failed to take with a cake
of lard and pumice. His nightshirt
printed on with a coal rake.

In the dream,
I'm alone on the abandoned
road, up in the orchards
hours before you'd reach Los Angeles—
an old Mercedes sedan thinks I'm hitching
and stops—   I climb in
and *here* it is like a parlor—   black with silver—
the steering wheel
folds into a mahogany dash, two couples
sit in front facing
as in a train compartment, an older gentleman
is in the back where I sit,
with caution, beside him—   I'd recognized
the car is on cow-pilot
and this is the deep future
with few people alive on the open road…

These five blood-sucking vudras
with black lariats in their laps are sharing
oxygen tubes in a milky tank of Don Alverzo's
laughing gas.

They dropped me off
in the first town
without conversation—   it's
the Christmas season and mechanical carolers
are revolving in a church steeple—
this is sickening like a choir
of doves in a third-rate

biography of Geronimo,
in other words
in the only known biographies
of the apache—

who was a holy season himself
by most accounts…

A young scientist walks past
slide rules in his pockets
making snowballs with lumps of coal at the center—   he's
saying to his girlfriend
that he hopes to wake in the morning
with the sun on his face and an erection—
I'm hoping to wake
simply

with anything on my face
including an apache with a blade
for this seems to be a false bardo
of becoming—   the girlfriend singing

hoe the row, you salty dogs,
row the ho', my darlings…

    III

It is a newspaper mural of the second migration
with wild dogs urinating to the ten directions—
it is a secret framing of the night sky
at solstice
with an old woman giving birth to garnets
and some startled prince whose purple foreskin
has just been pierced with a yellow stylus
of cactus. His blood spits captions,
by example: *the sun grows feathers,*
the moon scribbles circles for three
nights, or the earth shakes
like a two-cornered hat.

Or simply the corn is black. The maestro
laughs in the bardo of state craft: raffle pups
vomiting six pumpkins onto the lawn:
a troubled teen with a blade of bone
and obsidian has sawed off his head—   a fountain
of blood as a caption
for aftertime and the grandmother. The spider
insists the flat loaves
of bread will feed a third of the village, all
the others, she says, are dead.

IV

for Ryan

Signor, the hydra-headed squash
that blossoms is a visitor
from the mouth of Orion—   the sun
now dictates
a chalky rose paint—
Joshua and Ezekiel, the dark sisters,

in gray dresses,
are mating like insects on the courthouse lawn,
the steeple's flat compass and carols
lift the shepherds
with bags of cloves pressed
to their faces
while navajo sheep are hurried along the street.
Unbelievably, they have escaped the crèche.

The sunset wind lifts the snow
back on its haunches like the wolves.

V

An old maestro
says that in his green chest
wolves are feeding on carrion.
He is happy to have reached the wilderness. He asks
if it is a strawberry soda-crème, lowing
suds of oxygen in the blood of his nose.
Children laughing at him.

Beethoven has closed his night diary. Forget
taking the stairs. *Signor,* please

forgive him

VI

for he played the margins
and lost a nephew. Apricots,
and a tennis match on grass
beside a dark kennel
with a handful of Dalmatians
like a grammar, *full stop.*
Not wolves. Full stop.

VII

The frail ghost in the burning opera house,
declensions of hail in a landscape of lakes
the maestro thinks are filling with his gall and urine.
A fat pickerel on his hook and line
and just five years of age—   his father
yells Ludwig just run like hell for the hills
laughing while the fish flies past birches—

shape-shifting wolves, apaches, following the boy full measure
into a watercolorist's version of a mirror
at Versailles.

Signor, enough. Sigh. Enough…
It is the time to die.

VIII

You must know the standard measures
for pendulum and mirrors.

The wind lifts
the snow and an occasional shuttlecock
across the lawns. You wanted
this formality? Bells
going off in the firehouse. And yet
just another dead maestro
with a squash blossom in his mouth.
And yet another meal of red potatoes
and trout for the concierge's daughter.
It's not enough that we are happy
for her. It's enough.
Trout and the trolley's bell
going off inside the burning firehouse. Enough.

In a Western Siberian Wood

The cold garden is a matchstick-
pegged cribbage of two simple rows.

Blackbirds with red jewels in their breasts
are laughing
at the mirror glass and snow with stucco marl
of yellow quartz—   a frozen brook,
the small airport's windsock,
the blond wood for the beans, a garden map
tacked to the cupboard—   a hinge
of politics for a poor farmer, lame
in his sixties and half-blind.

A flight of clouds dragging the day moon
into the black town with fresh water.

There's the voice of reindeer
in rut
reading loudly from some book,
a Russian to English dictionary his dead son
abandoned before being killed in Afghanistan.

Then in March the old man's two strokes—
he thought the lard especially cold
in the early morning lamp.
He was never more alone than in the stadia dark
under the Chernobyl sky—   how
he wonders does an old man feel nostalgia

for shit like that…
yet he does.

        The yeti does.

Yamantau Mountain

Above the snowy purple distance of Urals
there is the emptiness of the flower pole
that is the naked ecliptic without a single star—
lequel est dans la constellation
du Dragon—monde, merde—

it is a secret nuclear ledge of granite
with freight cars entering, exiting
the awful hill. A concession of walking
swastikas.

Lilith dwelt there for a morning
bathing in white soot.

Mr. Vladimir, I haven't, anymore, the stomach
for you, you idiot!

The Conversation

So I told the grocer, David, that my
poorly defined brimless hat
is the bridge to Jalaluddin Rumi's backcourt…
that's a sack of avocados and a heel of rye. Sipping
anisette from thimbles. The fish
sun dried…

I told him it's good
the book is *used*, has changed hands. The salmon
too. The ovoids, *three*…

Four is no more.
A plague of fleas. The sudden
odor of gunpowder, a wild black thistle
and two late summer storms approaching
a hastily arranged camp—   one green
tent and the cooling beach wagon. The lake's

dull face marbled with the sky.
The birds gone silent.
Through the trees bacon snapping
like a sudden rain on canvas—   an opening
of no real significance
fifty-five years past. Our mother's

friend, Julia, running
naked beyond the gray boulders. The hail
laughing with her,
my brother slamming shut the door

to the mustard-colored outhouse. The Great Dane barking,
bleeding in the goldenrod
an early April Easter morning. And Julia,
tall with yellow hair,
dead the week before of a prodigious leukemia.

The Buddha on the Road

It was a Roman road with red cypress.
He is slain, a heavy walnut
of quartz straight
to his eyebrow from a slingshot
of hemp and cowhide. *Well met,*
is what he thought. Dead before
he met the dust of the road. The sun's
torch on the suburbs of Antioch.
A buddha fallen to tainted pig
or a white river rock
on the highway to Damascus. A sun swelling.
Finally, just another prince
dead in the dust, and of—

of course he saw it coming.
You didn't. This familiar
bigotry of love.

A Winter Window

The cloak soaked in blood
must be burned.

The dull brass trombone
lost in some lake
announced sunrise
for twelve straight nights
of a darker Palestine.

The mirage of government men
sitting with their Italian wives
in heavy fur coats
smelling of ether and cigarettes,
these earliest rows
of a Vatican midnight communion.

An old stove flares
in a far standing cupboard.
And scribbled in soap on the larder window:
         ajax / aktivnyye meropriyatiya.

The snow on the morning ledge
is inclined sparrows
eating at a ridge
of reddish Egyptian bread.

The sky separates four old mariners
from a dog star—   magi

eating potato salad
pointing at the sun.

The human cloak must be
rolled in blood. And burned.

Yet another Christmas morning in the suburbs.

In the Age of the Mud-Toad-Leopard

for Christopher Burawa

Above the black cinching vines and half-moon
the night roost of wintering
turkey buzzards
deposits its own hillside snow
of rent and berry fowl
like a sloppy broken wing
that balances a memory
of blossoming dogwood…

Every season lived is an exotic postage
suddenly cancelled
against the brown paper remnant—
the box of beeswax
that arrived yesterday from Ecuador.

The policeman across the street
is moving his lips with the neighbor woman
over the drunken schoolboy who slept
in their rat's-nest hammock last night.
She woke him with a broom.
While this ghost advances her narrative
it seems the tired policeman
is mouthing the slowest movements
within the *Ave Maria*…

It's almost as if language is music, is
doing the breathing for him.
The neighbor's face gone purple.
There is a diagonal November mix
of rain and snow.

No one can conceal in anger
its ultimate confession. She believes
the criminal mind is everywhere
just like the africanized bees
that fell from the white branch into her sad brown wig
leaving her, this past January,
dead like a swollen log beside the road.

At First Sky in April

In Tehran, in the alleyway of a jail
they're shooting their children
high, in the back of the skull
because, with this approach, less blood
is spilled—   the Russian *cheka*
established this practice in basement showers
where naked aristocrats in endless
lines fell in the cold cascade,
their bodies dragged up coal chutes
to the canvas of idling trucks for the certain passage
to the lime pits of the poorly lit suburbs.

At night in these black potato fields,
the *cheka* posted guards to discourage starving dogs—
it was these boys who reported
on the trafficking ghosts even far
back into the stubble of the woods. One kid said
these phantoms looked
like broken kites dragging
along the ground in a fitful wind. There is
something absolutely credible about this account—

I mean, boys, in late March, thinking of kites, boys
with lice,
with their penises flooding with light,
lights tied to their rifle barrels with hemp, *a dog
yelps once, twice…*

A Song without Words

The fallen bird of the field
in death is swollen.
In the fresh mathematics they solve
for *the known.* A herd of buffalo
made of string
stampeding into the arranged yields
of ramshackle daisy and coarse ringlets
of rue.

The theoretical screw
loose is a woeful calculation
like so many dark clouds
spilling a gravid rain over the darkening
castle at Elsinore. A ghost
is the obvious consort to the uncle,
not his queen. That's

why they have put it in his ear,
a vial of dragon urine
down the silver trumpet.

Exit the ghost in just another
quarrel between brothers. In the newest arithmetic
the brass doorknob
is a Salvador Dali
tesseract of left breast of shadow
and a burnished armadillo
sucking milk from it.

I've taken the pledge and made donations of blood and sperm
to the other world
of Sumatra-Betelgeuse, also known
as Planet X.

The Black Sun
is an approaching cata-strophe
of hope, dignified
with loose women and buttons of adrenaline you must eat
like cookies at the two cooling pools of milk.

Homage to Sesshu (1420–1506)

for Mari

The tree is like fresh hives
on a woman's breasts, after eating
a ripe black pomegranate.

The ink of two roofs
is the lifting wings
of three crows eating
from the burst sack
   of rice and tiger worms.

The snow is snow.

The Aspirin Papers

for Sean

On the white lacquered radio from Manilla
something by Ravel that is so heavily illustrated
it has made you dizzy and nauseous. The tall villain
from the Kingdom has been shot through the eye
and your three-year-old daughter
paces before the muted hotel television
wringing her hands
and with half-breaths, murmuring,
"Oh, no, he must have had a mother. Poor man?
Oh, no!"

The dust storm outside is heavy enough to weigh
on you like a very wet snow.
On the phone you said that they lie to us so often
that now only we know the difference.

The wind works an old Tucson granary down the street
to degrees of something like a new silence,
Martian
and indifferent.
Jen asks if you couldn't open the window
just a crack and Amelia is still pacing the room
in the green strobe of the old television. Off.

The power goes off for a moment and there is a feint
of unconsciousness. Then all the engines of the world
turning on again. You look at your wife and say, "Why not."

Under a Tabloid Moon

I

A clear afternoon. Forgive me
like the brass loud horns
against the blinding snow of a hillside.

Cosmo Monkhouse has just begun to deliver
a eulogy over his very own corpse.
And smartly he just said it: *forgive me*.

Drifts of nitrogen
crossing his hallucination of an original savannah
bordered by a yellow swamp.

Basically, again, I will miss you.

II

The kitchen is cold and smelling
of burnt toast. A sweet and sickly odor.
A smell, I thought, like the parallel of baroque
trumpets. A send-off with a landscape you have never
            known. My
vision went cloudy, milk
with the salt of tears. I washed them
in your cold pond water. Laura said

not to let them
fill you with water like a balloon.
So I refused them. Later in the afternoon
you did also.

III

So, friend, you could have died on a prison island
of the Emperor Domitian. The radio
gone silent.
The bridle tack on the locust,
at Patmos, gone gold and black
in a setting sun—

the portal light, on your darkening face,
now, a rose light on a sinking
freighter: thousands of swifts
flying from the rusted bulkheads.

The tabloid newspaper read:
dead, 13 Bengal tigers.

The Butterfly House

The last time I was here, a
year ago, the barn
held some garden furniture
that had been down by the lake
for too long—   it all crossed
in a dream
with a yellow table and chair
from our childhood; it all combined
to return our grandmother
to life—   she was cooking
a pot roast
in a brass pressure cooker
and there was a thunderstorm
over the mountain,

it was growing dark as night. I loved my grandmother's
parakeets, gone
silent with the thunder
now rattling the parlor cupboards—
in this dream the birds
were reading Kierkegaard
aloud to grandmother's favorite
dead seminarian. His hands

were in his lap: he hated storms. A tall naked girl walks up
out of the grass
with a small bowl
full of lake water and pours it
over his long black hair.

Neither of their bodies
have ever been recovered
from among the water lilies.

A brass pressure cooker and two parakeets
begin again their conversation.
                    The older bird
lamenting the loss of a white shoelace.

Hail shoots from the black cloud bank
above the lake.
My grandmother's apron drifting to the floor.

Flames breaking blades in the fieldstone fireplace.

4

Jericho Radio

for Sam Pereira

I

One coffee tin with grease in it, the other
with inky fists of turquoise—the faded
calendar page: platinum, rose
buttocks, a lens
of runoff, the snow again
on the mountain—two goats
in repetitive motion, night
pulse where the whistle on a steam
locomotive fills the valley
with absolute contour and volume.
The Leonids sparking a nostalgia
on the old Hayden's Ferry telegraph
and a long dead cat hears it.

The pastel awning of a Veteran's Day
saying, *the Leonids*
are not important.
You know. Or men
fake orgasms also. Broad snow on the Estrellas.
Another winter shoe of cold.
You should apologize to your physical corpse,
like Cosmo Monkhouse did,
then spilling the chamber pot,
reaching for his bowl of tea.

Not the sun-yellow grocery across the street
from the veterinary hospital, but
I'm buying boxes of frozen fish, and
frozen asparagus. Thinking my cat
has slowed with diabetes, I now know
that she is dead before the sun can set.
Between us there is rush hour
desert traffic
with dangerous pinball flubber
rain falling across it. Here, sudden rain
leaves them nude and confused,
more envy of schoolboys.
They are cradling slimy pods the size of day moons.
Weingarten called it the vaccination moon.
Our friend, Kenneth, is already dead
of mystery in Mexico. *I know.*
But he had to age
before he could get away with it.

III

The Chinese laborers forced to accept
a freight train in a snowy mountain pass
for that prayer you wake from
in an opium paralysis,
a faded calendar page, saying
wake again, fool, it is Bastille Day
and they're going to shoot
at that big stupid fuck De Gaulle
again. Lyndon Johnson eating
a banana split
in a cracked porridge bowl

in the darkening office.
The sad and pathetic child. At least
he was honest
like a boil on a goat
or a morning apocalypse
followed by a rainbow with azure lemonade filling it.

August Storm before the Hippodrome

Three plums snuggle along the ridge—
on the highway the ghost of ferocious
trucks in relay
appear as peppered dice on a cliffside—

the traffic flows so quickly it seems
stilled, at last, with rubies and diamonds
and a lack of yellow gas
in lines of simple folk
fleeing a coming hurricane
named Luke—   a comic book hero
saunters through the traffic in pajamas,

he has granted protection to three snowy owls
who now lift into the blacker clouds
as if seeding them with a nudity
and seafaring that are
by necessity more in keeping, Pacal,
with the birth of some infant
than, say,
the labor of its saintly mother
named Morning Star?

Butter

A Frenchman has taken
his nervous bank with him to the beaches
of Spain, from a glass-louvered bottom
of a small yacht he watches the vaulting ribs
of a sunken ship emptied
of the marigolds of salad
and dominion. His girlfriend's
breasts are copper; he will
sell, he thinks, his dead father's
dairy farm in late September.
Septembre. Septembre.
He is honestly reading a short story
by Poe. Thunderheads
moving over the lighter casino clouds
of mid-morning. He wonders
about Samuel Beckett
at late-night rehearsals.
Spear points and bullwhips
up in the darkening sky. Who wants to die
in springtime with a collapsed market
and in Paris. He laughs
having just bought back the farm. The slang
of the Americans gaining on him.

A Military-Academic Complex

The simple wind shear off plutonium petticoats
and up in a rioting air, thirty-three thousand
greek centimeters from Earth— the bozo belle aircraft
docking for fuel at the sock hop
for interdisciplinary storms
N by NW— or big sister innocently
feeds high-octane fumes
to a sweet meat of hurricane pecans.

Servings for up to eight Eskimos,
mechanics in the Enigma Four vestibules, black tin
hangars where the graffiti reads:
you flyboys will be the death of us.

Cold War nostalgia and X-rays of the thorax.
Oppenheimer in the hall corridor coughing…
the astronaut's gold-plated crucifix
in the adulterous bed of white knuckles—

marque nueve, allahu akbar, in midair
between tenements the choppers wash
off the long-faced bird's nest, machine-
guns splattering through the window box
of azaleas, at midair, sweeping
gunpowder, north/northwest… a locust-faced
helicopter…

not william burroughs fresh from posing
in the coffee shop, fresh

from the coast of Mexico
having gainfully shot
his dead wife in the addam's-apple. A whole generation's meek
inheriting a brown heroin off the night street.

Even the eight-foot-tall sotted mouse
in flight from the gringos thinking
she is dangerous peoples?

The flamingo knitting needle buried
in the eye of suspicious passivity. The ghosts?
The ghost queen of Monaco saying
well if those flyboys have the flu
everything is still possible.

Winter Melons

Sparrows, swallows, and swifts like crushed
flying or simply weighted *x*'s
and *w*'s of strict clockwork
streaming from a half-sunken freighter
with freshly colored Egyptian palette stamps.
The smoke from the bulkheads
a bargaining in crisis…
A big boom over by the park,
another
just beyond the airport. You almost look up
but persist there at the table
reading from the menu
written in archaic French. That
crazy Russian pip-squeak has opened the air
above Yamantou Mountain. Forget it.
A global cat's cradle of fine smoke.
Forget it. The fucking French. Fucking Russians.
Who could ever trust them.

The Last Light of a Quantum Plenum

Love has no body and presides the sun.
JOHN BERRYMAN

The shadows are falling out of the trees
acquiring a night sky
for eyes—
paper holding hands in chain
and the small cloud walking
that bows to a nursery of suns,
to the velvet underbelly of cosmos.

A simple sunset stands
for repetitions of last light in an arbitrary
fullness from, of course, *an outside-
looking-in.*
The superstitions of a bearded science
scolding us for our advantages of heart and mind.
All their darker texts defeated with yet
another canceling twilight—   it's no mystery, suffering
an alphabet in numbers
that has poisoned finally our air, the water, and the children.

The Boat

You kissed me sweetly on the bald spot
of my head—   your lips
cold with tea
you had been drinking all morning.
You said your eyes hurt—   that the tennis ball
was colored that weird green
so to be visible
above the clay court but not
in the long grass beyond the fence.
You said your eyes had shellac
on them. You have two
whiskers growing from your chin.
You remember still the photograph
of smiling African children
who did not ride the riverboat
that burned
terribly beyond the swamp in March.
You thought maybe two more weeks
of this and the long Labor Day
weekend and then you'd wish
we were all dead. Not the whole
fucking planet. Just our country
and two or three others thrown in…

Sif Mons & the Messenger Birth Star

It's the indigo saliva and methane
wrung with the goose's neck, a nineteenth-century
printer with his loose apron
leaves the perfect thumbprint
in the snow of the goose breast.

That night, with a loaf of bread
and an armful of crayon flowers, he
sidesteps the sweep's rain
of ashes. His wife
has made a yellow pudding.
He has inked three pages of young
Keats's *Endymion*. His head
aches. An insolvent tooth,
small brass pliers focusing on it.

The bliss of the night churning
its poor plasma and smoke—   a draft
down the barn's aisle
where he stands to piss
admiring the new glistening foal,
thinking how easeful it is
being a modern man with a sack
of cabbages and pork and an early winter sky
clear past the fallen linden bridge
and the north fork in the road
with a small dark cloud
and a white thumbprint in it.

Tiflis. July 1931.

So Mandelstam would grow oranges
in a glacier. I can hear
his cough beyond the drifting snow.

Candles, three,
in a row guttering like spam.
You heard his coughing
beyond
the sudden rattling of the petrol cans.

Bad teeth are a kind of sermon...

The prisoner train coughing
across the Turkish hills.

An Egyptian postage stamp
on his forehead, he shoots
at flying red squirrels, laughs
and misses again...
some nasty tobacco and gin
from the old woman polishing spoons.

Osip asleep in an electric arc
like the open boat
with a black canister of Saltines
and currant jelly.

What does the one have to do
with the other—   a marginal cash

note to the widow
details nothing.

Nothing and its red mustache. Coughing?

Again

I'd left Paris for the beaches
in Spain. I'd sold
my dead father's farm
and, in shame,
bought it back again
at a great loss...   then
a plough found
a shelf of bismuth
and I sold just the north pasture
for big serial profits
and I am ashamed again:
the huge white bones of my father's
favorite cow exposed
one late September morning!

It's always been potatoes and bread
or millions of francs on speculation.
I am not stupid. I'm not dead.
But the bones of an old cow assemble
repeatedly now in a dream
where my naked lame father
sits in a tub of boiling milk
and screams at me
first my name and then his name
which *is* the same

name. The crimes of the verb *to be*
pushing a hard rain in general
across the city and its suburbs...

The Oral Tradition

I

The three schoolgirls wait in the snow
for their bus,
or the mother's yellow beach wagon.

II

I, too, am a child, actually an X-ray
of a small child's chest.
During the winter, my best friend contracted polio.
Her father burned all her linen
in a red barrel under the elm trees.

III

A not at all anxious Israelite
with a jeweled breastplate
is carrying a clay tablet
through the rooms of our house.
When he passes my bed I see
sparrows flying
from a nearly sunken freighter.

IV

I asked the Israelite
what is that thing he's carrying?
He says *don't be alarmed
it's just a wall switch—
on/off, off/on…*
I wake crying.

V

In an old bezel of wisdom
please understand the coincidence
of a large mirror resting flat
on darkly polished floorboards.
The frame of the mirror and the wood
of the floor are indistinguishable
one from the other.
A pearly wet light everywhere!

VI

When
on the wall, the mirror is closed.

VII

The simple first plane of spirit
is not extensive, it is
switchback after switchback.
The mountain

is collapsed as with the mirror
but, yes, with zippers like a human skull.

VIII

A chosen one's large head
touches his sister's feet
while they travel
down the birth canal
into a bath of midnight light
from a sooty lamp.
This is Tibet. There's a plague
and conifers.

IX

It is deliberate like the fish
slapping the floor
of the black reed boat.

X

One bone of this fish,
called the Elias bone,
is stuck in the throat.

XI

Washing your face in cow urine.
A turnstile
of light. A table set
with bread and wine:

one bone of this fish,
called the Elias bone,
is stuck in the throat
of the fish

XII

like a compliment
of mirror glass or a simple
switch of birch
across your hands and face
being washed in cow urine
as a disinfectant…

beside the seven lakes.

Last Published by Fire on the Pages of Lament

The old painter telling the yellow nude on the sofa
to move if she must while he warms
his arthritic elbow in the steam of a boiling macaroni.
He blames her discomfort on a loose organization
of willows along the cold river. Birds screaming
their relevance at him. A handful
of colored chalk flying past her slow hairbrush.
The wind knocks again at the door like some horseman
bringing sealed documents, the new warrants of spice merchants
in the flooded city.
You don't want to ask when any of them
have last eaten. The birds again screaming
from the dark ledgers of high dry-closets.
Just an early spring and these fourteen strict lines

of some unearthly tolerance warming her blue fingers
in the red hairs of her crotch like an unwanted written ornament.

At the Tomb of Naiads

Deep in the woods, a small horse
with ice
like black tackle in its gray mane
eats the fresh snow.

Two white keys
on a piano are struck at once
and the horse lifts above the trees.

The stars are signaling to me.

I am so sick
of the miraculous creatures
settling in their red beds of floss.

There's the unfiltered Pall Mall
Eisenhower would have put
in the mouth
of a dying gunnery sergeant
who smiles
there in the snow
with a big orange moon sitting
in the pines.

He coughs. And that crazed shit Hitler
is dead. I am born
somewhat egocentric
with my mother's blood on my shoulders. Now

Hiroshima beads up
in the white slick on my small stomach.
Everyone grows shy
for a quarter of a century. They eat pie—

the aliens are arriving
in silent silver cigar cases
to observe the mass extinctions.

I was born in candlelight
in a late winter thunderstorm.
I begin to eat snow. More ships
leaving the Pleiades
to visit our equator.

And furthermore
several nuclear wars
have been averted
like the eyes of the Naiads
eating the snow that the dogs have yellowed…

5

A Fifteenth-Century Bishop in His Lavender Mummy Cloth

The bruised boy in the mudroom
is obligated
to the mantis posture of a pine sawhorse
and a sponge of vinegar.
Owl is the bishop's name. The cannon pendulum,
battery of lambs, is his game.
Again, and again.

He was the deliberate genius of the honeypot,
wet cinnabar script, skip-cipher
of acrostic verse, not on the margin
of Leonardo's black mirror. (Crossed
sentences of ammunition
belts on the chest of a bobbing
Mexican horseman.
A tea-revolution of candy skulls.
The long rain calendar of white umbrellas.)

On the darkening robe
sprays of iris and semen. The hot iron
crease runs from his face
through the burial sheet
into a high loft of coughing sopranos
who are now bearing daggers into the streets
and who, nevertheless, assert their love of us
and of the infallible blank
that is coitus.

Shakespeare

The wigmaker's daughter squats under the gray
oak tree, nervously looking
beyond the road while she pees…   he

reads the burial lime brought here
against disease, the finches tracking
it over red slate, it approximates

the shorthand scribbling
of the pirate publisher's stenographer
in the shadowy pit of the Globe Theatre:

he hates all these thieving birds
by extension
to the vile clerks
whose strange company he keeps; ask
the flesh-and-blood pensioner-king
whittling along the stream at hamlet's mill.

Where does it come from? Who knows.
The smell of bear shit and blood moving
across the stage from the adjacent baiting gardens.

He told his landlady
his chamber pots and her eyeballs
both need fanatical polishing. He feels
mostly lost. A new century for confusion.

The man is fully resentful at morning rehearsals.
Burbage cakes white talc to the face,
looks up at a charwoman who screams into the street,
all the ciphers of birds stirred by her feet,
the poet says *cogitating sugars*
leading to a church. Shit,
he thinks, I'll be lucky to live out the week.

Gotterdammerung

There was, I think, a garnet irritant in the powder
and so I took a pill against it
and fell unconscious there in the heaps
of cosmetics—   the approaching horns
of the hunters with slow livery, all opera
like water turning with the stag
turning to a dragon. The mist moving off
the river and Brunnhilde with a blue torch
walking asleep among the wharfs. The metropolitan

insisting that the stage
was being prepared for me, someone
sweeping sawdust, glitter, and an ankle
with foot, living and dead mice—
if the world was burning, it was
Damascus I visited: two men hanging
from a very green tree, hanging
by their feet and the children
collecting coins beneath them.

Brunnhilde with her breasts cut off and red-faced dogs
barking from the cavities. Her voice
has become the river. I wake
with flames in all my joints. My hands swollen—
minutes later they are sawing
the gold ring from my black finger.
My husband watches with the lolling tongue
of the stag, more dogs hanging from his groin

and throat. I said
to the nurse, *Elizabeth*
had a dress that was soaked in poison?

The Mirror

for Richard Howard

We dream of two dragons
conflicted in a wilderness.
It is only the spatial instance
of a luckless accidental order
that says "horse" rather than "house"
but also
says "horse"
rather than "aqueduct."

These, all in the same moment,
spontaneous or
immeasurably meek.
As if under a cloak
of nearness or inevitability
like two suns become one.

It is not belief but
an attraction
to an experience we hunger after,
here and now, an almost
self-annihilating
difference become common, beyond
fear.

If you have changed water to wine,
you will soon
turn wine into tears.

In a Matter of Adders

circa 2012

The liege lord heavy with black furs
is crossing the fields of mud and snow
with no apparent rose
hovering against the turquoise horizon
where in early April the burial boat
with his mother's corpse,
with fraught possessive punctuation,
returned from France. He said
shit in italic
into the west wind and wiped
his nose along the muskrat sleeve
clear past the elbow.

His oldest daughter misses her the most
and will only eat old unleavened
bread with water
from the well that's been
compromised by the last sea surge
that flooded the potato yard at Christmas.

She now is looking sickly.

We *should* forgive this man who never
ever forgave anyone, or thing?

Of course, we don't. In fact,
fuck him and the red
counterfeit sun his favorite painter
placed on a large canvas

that must first be lacquered
with a thin paste of rabbit fat,

the rabbits' screams
reaching our lord who, in nonchalance,
is crossing cold dark fields
calling to his mother's ghost—
she who on her last day
hemorrhaged like a rose, fold

after fold.

Speech of the Paraclete's Mouse

The smoke from the garden-house window
went unnoticed in Rome
because of a diesel marmalade
that is the evening air…

the fleshy orangutan sun dropping its summons
to play billiards in an open-air theater
of boiling macaroni and barbeque.

The woman nursing her twins
shifts them onto her shoulders
so they might express suds,
while her breasts
just continue to shoot milk
into the street where two cats
are realizing the frontiers of happiness.

The black van crushing only one of them,
yes, *the lucky one*.

The twins
nursing again. Their fingers playing
something like Scriabin in quick concert
to the pigeons

The pigeons saying, *"I'm starving, I'm starving—*
Thank you very much, thank you very much—
Fuck you, too.

Aren't you my first
sister's cousin?
Shut up! Thank you very much."

The Solar Famine of Hansel and Gretel

It was like Hopi on the edge
of a cliff shitting into
the oceanic mother dark…
I don't know why
but last night
I was eating spaghetti
with ten big firemen.
Then within this dream
I dreamt that

I watched
while three Stone Age women
silently left a cave
to actually squat and pee
on the cold white lip
of a newspaper rock, not
really awake,
all three women just
staring into and beyond
the fog and drizzle of early morning.

In the fire station
three large pears rested
on the kitchen sill,
the window fogged with the old Kenmore
dishwasher.

Then the pole
alarms and suspenders went *on/off…*

A black fire up in the mountains.

Ur-Dream

for Mila

The night sky is a desperate
clump of blue dye.

The mountains are like mirrors
in an ocean liner
draped with snow and ice.

This inland sea is lime green
to please someone
other than me. The sandy cove
is mustard with a stone boat
that is a fossil of walrus.

The other boat is a thin slice
of amethyst trash. *Light
dancing on its teeth.*

I push it out
over the smooth waters. A creature
now wakes on the beach,
a Klee triangle of spring jade
for a beard. There's

a sack of buttons somewhere
and someone sings
who is boiling
water for the silver thermos of tea.

For Tranströmer

In the cold heavy rain, through
its poor lens,
a woman
who might be a man
writes with a can of blue paint
large numbers
on the sides of beached whales—

even on the small one who is still
living, heaving
there next to its darkening mother
where the very air is a turnstile...

I'm certain this woman is moved
as anyone would be—
her disciplines,

a warranted gift to us,
to business, government,
and our military,

and still she exhibits care and patience
this further
talent for counting,

counting...

"The Sparrow"

The little Blaisdale girl was knock-kneed
and cranky with freckles. She was
quiet and often immersed
in the King's versions of holy writ.
They called her Sparrow,
so the Lord would be watchful of her…

When her father's boat failed
to come back from the North Atlantic
there was finally a memorial
followed by a feast—
she and I were charged
to take blue enamel kettles
full of garbage
out to the pit beyond the henhouses.

She was a year older than me and could
walk faster. I stumbled
twice in the pigs' run. It was
a cold peninsula in Maine.

It was snowing heavily…

In her old communion dress she was
now invisible in a white wind—   the gulls
arriving were quickly lost
also in the storm:
there was a disembodied sobbing, only the red
carapace of lobsters, the screams of gulls

and then again,
only the armor of those big sea spiders
climbing high to a vanishing point
beyond even Butler's Cove
and the great granite face
of Morse Mountain which like a freighter
from Asia moved impossibly into the nor'easter…

Asia was where her mother said the father
had died first,
eating even the bones of snakes, the sound
of gnashing teeth
there beside the compost heap, again and again,
with full ardor
and in the full circle of cold and nitrogen.

The Crop Circle of a Country Parson

It is all light footwork
with old boards, knotted swanks
of greasy rope; the compass nail
is my hayloft pike, sill manure
from the cows' parlor caked to it.

You must dance as if in a field
of snakes. But all the while
the dull silk sputum of spiders
is rising, diagrammatical phantom
volunteering in the dark
salt fields of the mind…

There's a thousand petals
of rose and emerald, the trousseau of our Lady,
her skirts between the teeth
crossing quickly a white winter stream.

The blasting in my brain,
with a shadow line like a milky quasar,
is a strobe again
of rose quartz, *then,*
a rush of molten lead climbing
for the heart, four petals
lowering, groaning
like drawbridges at the top—
the night sky filling my eyeballs.

To think that warm ale, a boy's hoax,
and the arrogance
of a morality inseparable
from science should yield
a sacred compunction for geometries
in a migraine that would blind
a king in the act of killing a king: the

intestines wrapped around a chubby jeweled wrist
and a sharpened lip of chalice
chopping out the heart. That was the first thought
in watery barley
after finishing a bright isosceles
angle like some jawbone out of Ecclesiastes.
I'm well lost

is the long and short of it. My wife
would drown me in a sack of nails
like a sick dog. It was
her most generous thought. Blue triangles
of light in steady distances
above the hill, then, as she put it,
streaming off into Orion
like a cluster of soiled carrots dragging
a blue burning mop handle
she'd like to stick up my ass
twice.

The First Light of a Quantum Plenum

for Hannah

I

The sun paints the obsidian blade, a green
quarreling with liver...   the Olmec
cross on the hillside
like a pink-black bird over a plague city.

One in twelve Jesuits missing fingers
on the gloved hand,
digits fitfully sawed off
with tiny white shells
by North American savages...   *more sums
over histories,* a predictability of sun
not trusting the pus and gauze of empire.

Mexico City and Montreal shake...

II

> *we do not enough attend
> to what passes within...*
> PERCY BYSSHE SHELLEY

The madness starts here saying
time was once just another dimension
of space, stilled and nearly solid, then
provoked again into movement: splitting
burly cathodes, silled and projective. The lamp
of privilege that gets to ask the question.
Albert, do you still

love the one glove of entanglement? What are
the ten biggest banks in Argentina?

He doesn't refuse the confusion of little
red sleigh bells in the passing big hair
of the very small woman walking out of water
in a graying Berlin.

The madness starts here with the patent
on an active unspeakable
refrain…   a turquoise piano
filled with ice cubes. Gin in their shoes. Again.
Not Germany, but a geology

past redemption, it was
literally bound to happen to us,
the infinite condition of rigor
in a breeze, in *that* stand of trees!

(The Planck satellite blinking off in some
quick inflation, a fairy tale now
in the burning frontier ramparts, a failed
ramshackle mathematics calling
Taxi, taxi-loon…

The hermitage redistricting across the microwave
background of yellow donkeys.)

This Arab winter selling matches in the streets.

III

Love, the question is about burnt meat and potatoes.
An ethical meal of bone. In the smaller quotations
of bone.
Naked, she pushes
aside the fried potatoes and jam.

Someone in television arguing that the beauty
of a woman's breasts is classical.
Just perfect nonsense rising into trees
beyond my balcony. A reminder
of the kite up in the big linden.

My cat's been dead now for two weeks.

IV

That ragged kite is my right bivouac,
a paper hinge of existence
lodged in the darker branches.
The cat watched it like colored

strangely dimensional pages
turning toward the sullen ferry
bobbing out on a nearly frozen lake
with folds of fading water, lots
of blood in the sputum.
Our sun
an undiscovered sunken riverboat
of margarine.

It's a simple matter
of how much importance

you'll assign to a discreet molecule
that has never met you. And
that wouldn't ever want to...

This silence is for Shelley. His wife's
chin was thought to be blunt
but classical. I miss
them both like a toothbrush.

Or pair of sandals.

v

It's like those ignorant Italian fisherman
plunging their long, sharpened poles
deep into the beach sand
hoping to find the hastily buried corpse
of the drowned Shelley. The widow
protesting...

Suddenly a much different sound,
not more *da-woush,*
but something modern, a wet sand,
skin, thigh bone! Birds screaming up and off

the pinking cliffs. Our government
weaponizing viruses...   miles
of open trenches
from the hedgerows to the sumptuous sea.

Notes

"The Fallen Bird of the Fields" is dedicated to the memory of Susan Albright.

I believe "British Petroleum" is reckless with a fact regarding the lives of P.G. & H.C.?

"The Novel as Manuscript" is for Spencer Hanvik.

"Joan of Arc" is dedicated to John-Michael Bloomquist.

"The Last Light of a Quantum Plenum" is dedicated to the memory of Mr. Hummingston.

"Sif Mons & the Messenger Birth Star" is dedicated to Paul Cook.

"Again" is dedicated to Ryan Holden.

"Last Published by Fire on the Pages of Lament" is for Fritz Goldberg.

"At the Tombs of Naiads" is written in memory of Steve Orlen.

"A Fifteenth-Century Bishop in His Lavender Mummy Cloth" is for Hugh Martin.

"For Tranströmer," in adaptation, is a song by Spencer Hanvik and Norman Dubie.

About the Author

Norman Dubie was born in Barre, Vermont, in April 1945. His poems have appeared in many magazines, including *The American Poetry Review, Bombay Gin, Crazy Horse, Gulf Coast, Narrative, The New Yorker, Paris Review,* and *Poetry.* He has won the Bess Hokin Prize from the Poetry Foundation and fellowships from the Ingram Merrill Foundation, the John Simon Guggenheim Memorial Foundation, and the National Endowment for the Arts. *The Mercy Seat: Collected and New Poems* won the PEN Center USA prize for best poetry collection in 2002. He has published with *Blackbird*, a book-length futuristic work, *The Spirit Tablets at Goa Lake.* He lives in Tempe, Arizona, and is a teacher at Arizona State University.

Poetry is vital to language and living. Since 1972, Copper Canyon Press has published extraordinary poetry from around the world to engage the imaginations and intellects of readers, writers, booksellers, librarians, teachers, students, and donors.

WE ARE GRATEFUL FOR THE MAJOR SUPPORT PROVIDED BY:

THE PAUL G. ALLEN
FAMILY FOUNDATION

Anonymous	Gull Industries, Inc.
John Branch	on behalf of William and Ruth True
Diana Broze	Mark Hamilton and Suzie Rapp
Beroz Ferrell & The Point, LLC	Carolyn and Robert Hedin
Janet and Les Cox	Steven Myron Holl
Mimi Gardner Gates	Lakeside Industries, Inc.
Linda Gerrard and Walter Parsons	on behalf of Jeanne Marie Lee

WE ARE GRATEFUL FOR THE MAJOR SUPPORT PROVIDED BY:

Maureen Lee and Mark Busto

Brice Marden

Ellie Mathews and Carl Youngmann
as The North Press

H. Stewart Parker

Penny and Jerry Peabody

John Phillips and Anne O'Donnell

Joseph C. Roberts

Cynthia Lovelace Sears and
Frank Buxton

The Seattle Foundation

Kim and Jeff Seely

Dan Waggoner

C.D. Wright and Forrest Gander

Charles and Barbara Wright

The dedicated interns and faithful
volunteers of Copper Canyon Press

TO LEARN MORE ABOUT UNDERWRITING COPPER CANYON PRESS TITLES,
PLEASE CALL 360-385-4925 EXT. 103

The Chinese character for poetry is made up of two parts: "word" and "temple." It also serves as pressmark for Copper Canyon Press.

The text is set in Aldus, a typeface designed by Hermann Zapf. Sans serif display type is Scala Sans by Martin Majoor. Book design by VJB/Scribe. Printed on archival-quality stock.